JARED STANLEY

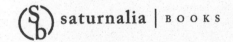

saturnalia | BOOKS

Distributed by Independent Publishers Group
Chicago

Saturnalia Books
2816 North Kent Rd.
Broomall, PA 19008
info@saturnaliabooks.com

ISBN: 9781947817647 (print), 978-1-947817-65-4 (ebook)
Library of Congress Control Number: 2023943690

Cover art by Caitlyn Galloway
Book design by Robin Vuchnich

Distributed by:
Independent Publishing Group
814 N. Franklin St.
Chicago, IL 60610
800-888-4741

SO TOUGH

The green catch of light your eyeglasses get

basic enthusiasms where the flowering grasses nod in the wind

another cruel ongoingness

fell asleep with a cock-shaped bookmark on my eyes

the sea is off somewhere by itself

previously unimagined inhabitants of spume

blood in your mouth did you taste it

This summer touches my face oddly.

The hot gore of its afternoons

dries the blood to a powder. It's not so wild,

every age finds an intricate suffering—

this one has thirst and particles in summer.

Some half-remembered folk melody cries out

for gallon jugs of green river wine:

tastes like grass, fucks you up, cold on the tongue

Dear voices fill a room beyond the wall

fill my ear, my cup, so far for us to go

undersea, aboveground, feeling

       for a level surface upon the earth

the timbres, the changes, lovely, in accordance

barely vibrating these bones

little half-moons of smokelight

in the typewriter keys

Singing close to the ground

light tastes like air, kinda

touched, felt by other generations

"bright nests in nests"

my hope, it will be air plus music

touch a dry grass stalk, it's whole

to shoeless feet

they don't seem like great distances

I.M. Jean Valentine

North of here, smoke from distant fires

rises over the ridge, blows closer all the time

holding shadows at an angle

to no one's surprise and everyone's grief

the earth shakes loose its mammoth stones

wiggling the treetops as it does.

What happened here? The trees laugh. *Nothing!*

they say, *we're just screaming!* Life is a dream of them

And I fill each line with jewels, blanks

fine straw, the grasstips drooping,

a gust slips down past my loose, ornamental

parenting style, a purple aura

from a drop of tangerine juice

motion and no motion, enthusiasts of

Thursday, heh, it's very Thursday

everyone's drunk and nobody's thirsty

The shooting began in San Jose on a day like this one

at a time like this, the poets were laying low on

the heavy, uneven ground, dry lips beneath the weather

(any exposed bit turns into leather) looser than a bullet.

Is there a deliberate way to wear an earthbound look, warm

but not too warm, to put on a woozy disaster like a shirt?

Able-bodied youths throw their muscles at smoke.

It's Sunday: time to feel free in a house

If there is a future and we get to be wise creatures within it

wearing perhaps a nice tunic, caftan, or sport coat

pushing boats upstream with our thoughts

the capital destroyed, such things we had seen

ash rained down on the city of fun

a gnat swims around my eye

the children mistake whatever this is for snow

the sand in our teeth tastes bitter but we get used to it

Healing was this small thing we had

unemotional, and all emotion

I wanna be your shirt, I wanna fit you

I'll be your coast, grown bare in the windrush

Bashō's weather-beaten skeleton

(he always wrote about fleas)

a bonfire in the rose garden

survival plants of the East Bay

Rain drips into the neighbor's green pool

clear water into green water

a swish of fuzzed hair down the edge of your jaw.

Reclining like this, no future is a future

where some prefer only the best world-class

creams and balms to rub on a dry foot

with a bleating squirt of mellow cruelty—

everybody else gets vigils, vigils, a future of vigils

Of the stash of new wave records from the Savers on Kietzke

and the hissing dust in a cold tune on side one of *The Psychedelic Furs*

and that unending, preternatural click I detect when the record skips

and the speck or mote from the sleeve stings the rim of my eye

and the sweat dripping on my tattoo of Caligula's garden of delights (Oh, time!)

plus the outrageous bills for mom's nursing home and granola bar habit

and the glistening faith of a summer lawn in a drought

deftly impersonal like the first part of grief: let in the cool air when while you can

This voluptuous shirt of air

tousled gusts of fuck

the rhythm of payment

unwinnable style

bite marks on the wind's back

a panoply of distorted fart noises

I get so lazy and wanton

a good time, a blue dude

I confess to the study of clouds

to loving the mysteries

distrusting the wound

a crust of salt upon the slipping rock

for your feelings

I'm doing this, trying

to test what light tastes like, lick two tears

one swarms with intertidal green

Orange moon nudges the play structure

buteos and accipters

hover and swoop in a future of suffering

wads, ashes, and swathes

        the morning cool turns

while the foxtails brush the surface

my heart's too cold for this heat—

You keep saying that, burning up

Skunks live in the drain by the parking lot

the dream police haunt my standing here

lungs in Pompeii, lungs in plaster

walking out into the green, escapist drizzle

a storm drops cool hells our way

no cleansing tremolo fell like rain today

to collect the ash and lay it on the earth

the ground could open at any time

It was a years-long return

to our home beneath the mountain

no need to waste a flag on the place

mud on a claw mark, burnt coffee on a shirt

another summer with the smoke map—

we tripped over roots to get here

toward the oaks in our unmarked arrival

it feels soon over here, maybe soon

Here you are on the Galata bridge eating a fish sandwich,

your face changing shape in the dusk light off the Golden Horn

here you are in Reno, your shoulders' red tracery

where the sun came down to say *fuck off*

here you are in Philadelphia, someone I can only imagine

in a red hoodie among the springlike dormancy of the world

here you are in Berkeley, after dancing all night at Li Po Lounge,

stumbling back across the bridge, a bit of lipstick on your tooth

Trash cans huddle in the lower arches

of the Theodosian walls

neighborhood kids hold up

anonymous fragments of bread

say *hello,* wealth is gross, this rain is intense

vines curl out of masonry

put some flesh on eternity

a pigeon in the hollow of a high window

Since it's Monday, stay loose about the goddam facts.

If you're busy flowering into your circumstance

and animals should fall from chiseled letters in a cloud

read the blur and sigh, sip from the stranger's cup,

get a good angle on it and suck. It's easy as

feeding your heart to a dog in a heat wave or

drawing a great half-moon in the margins of a sea:

air combs a finger over the miraculous pool

When the tree smoke gets in my lungs

I like to squint at the world—

these teeny scuds of clairvoyance

kinda haze my inner eye, make a suck

suck sucking whoosh up the ashen ectoplasmic

wildfire's face—it's very floaty up here

this world we just started to think of and burn in

an insane amount of heat and ashfall

Let this personhood waft and crest

—maybe wander or puff up, blossom

a small bump: curved and available, cool

as a microspore twirling up my face…

isn't *that* something to learn

not just horror or power,

any charm: and my unspeakable you

strays. I must be your child

I'm missing out

on so much!

They are friends

with gorgons,

werewolves, and—

oh, but you already

know about the

punk rock mermaids

Some life returns

at the approach of a stranger:

in the moving, furtive

disappearance the years are made of

my hands do all this weird shit:

looking for a changed shape of air

elusive agitations and sympathies

they cup your shoeless foot

You're very young, so you

need a rhyme near your heart

a bit of color to hum to yourself

after the cold dream cleaves

like a priceless trinket from a small(er) Antarctica

and microplastics in the glitter spangle

the fibers of your purple shorts—something

for when you're hurt, scuffed in year and wind

So alone, so tough

so weird at home, so weird in public

on the street a whiff of body spray

blows in off a stranger's shoulder

the look is human, *nameless to nameless*

the texture of a luxuriant shoe

if I keep my droplets to myself maybe

Wednesday will be a consolation

Take courage

or towering succor

these exquisite lights

pattern the walls in ruinous blue

fingertrace a disappeared

change in the spinning air.

Lost at heart, it's wonderful

whose lazy sigh brushes my ear

Palms down the canyon

graffiti a jewel-toned kerchief

dried-up bits of the imperium set

within the marvelous quail beeps. Fronds bend.

I can tell from your eyes, at a distance of miles

you feel a bit convinced. Can a ruin approach

the status of music, sound like a feeling

from this far, echo in this garden?

In the dry essentialism of the morning

let us recommit ourselves

to the way things knock together

let us lick one another's armpits

in the course of breathing

I send a greeting out to your solidity

before the burning pause of midday

you get in me and I gust up

How many times

can you write about ash

in the undersmoke?

The indicator light

on the air purifier is red:

to begin in ignorance with

the spirit of trust and to end

getting high on burning trees

Born of evaluation and measurement

I see right through you, April.

Sun kisses my brow like a boss

a skein of cotton half covers the eyes

the covetous skin, where letters form

sunspots on the glory of my face

bottle glass scattered in the leaves

I hold a slit of light from the eclipse

I open the book and feel fear

and fear people maybe seeing my fear

and see people feeling my fear.

Your body doesn't stop being

your body when you choose to be

in a dark room for several days.

Feel the ink with your hand:

you're ruining my book. I can hear you.

Off in the bushes with the unseen

dropping rocks through a spider's web

rustling with some tough giggles

whichever pain blots out curiosity

my windsucked vulture'll pluck it out

the oblivious hand is comfortable in thorns

an oblivious hand in a tangle

too physical for any Monday in this century

Soft liquid, rich cream, refreshing gel

Here, another book of suffering, this is for you

folded into an airplane and sent down, up,

thrashing in a thrashing wind. The earth makes a sound

a waggling tongue under the sod

cream-colored, soft, milled, and bendable like this one.

The light is getting pretty orange up here

lolling around in the tops of the firs:

I shiver all through my carbon

In the greasewood, the bitterbrush,

I crawl and walk, a lover scuffed

with refusals, scratches; the shade pulls at me

the suck of anger pulls, the cold-blooded

luck in nature: water tickles when it falls

into the rock, so I turn to you, cliff-

lichen-green, stone licked-with-gray: we're ok

sucking, spitting pebbles into the road

The moralizing pierce of the sun on the tip of my house

the look on the face of my hero's daughter

your peace on the edge of my nostril

A CLEAR SUBSTANCE OOZED FROM THE BUMP

goo with eyeballs going on about Ram Dass

an ill wind glitter-fucked with starlings

an oldness to this stretch of day

everybody but _____ knows what I mean

Hide from the sun

in balsamroot time

the light in its cunning

wants this skin to

pass over the blade

clean into me

the dark sky sanctuary

in black widow time

The cranky assholes of the intellect

become the cheerful dipshits of the will

the end of the world was just last year!

Phlox and chick lupine I don't care

and now it's Thursday, anyone

this one; air hums, moves through

the building and alongside the cheek.

Time to hold onto your methodical fascinations

A mountain is cleaved and grass is made to hiss in air:

everybody knows how light scatters across the backside

of the poem's inside voice producing phthalates

which are said to make sperm commit suicide:

eh, well, into the rock the water must fall—

that's just one way to feel weight, though no feeling

must be expressed until the signal is given:

I recognize your improvised devotion, the flower in your hair

When I get motherless

in the camellias

colors rot, greens fuzz

this gentle winter look

under the drought-sun flits more

green in dried stalks along the fence:

the world's peace for a resting tongue

quiet in the bottle glass, looser than sand

This one makes no sense in the future

which is Thursday; go eat a hamburger

hunt flies with a lighter

keep your eyes on the road, dude

scratch the implant they put in your neck

come, pull down thy mask, my camouflaged neighbor

go ask the distant bull-shaped cloud, phased with meaning

why thy gun droops in the street

January 6, 2021

Since Thursdays don't exist, I suffer little

but Dad, you're interested in impossible things

I find another hour, swab and tweez with classical patience

an undreamt-of sleep with total information

that humming building with the logo

had a lot of wind in its saying

leftover fortune cookies stop making sense:

The price of innocence is cruelty

In a meditative fear

a big, pictureless dollar bill

enjoys looking serene, is covered in barf

look at it resting on a bed of de-platformed biomass

what to do with such cruel peace

gentle thing, reader, test the stillness

a picture of the opposite world

we'll have to get there on foot

light-slashed ridges form a scorpion's tip

Northern light smears through the butter-yellow window

of this Nova Era, one of eight locations around Toronto (and York).

Gentle northern summer, I like it when you glisten on a frosted bun:

hard, sugary light like a rock to hide under (or bite).

I thumb an angelic design in bubbles, steam rises from a burnt pot.

It's too much. Correct or corrected or correctable,

types of things stretch beyond the greased light of a cake shoppe.

The giant weight of any *them* in clean shoes, scuffing the top of an earth

The year had been looking for its vigil

as winter poured out

found me leaning on her pillow

on the brim of her pain, my child

her face loosened, half-lit,

a night-shape bent toward morning.

Last week, the pities were outside

this week, like purse candy, they're stuck in here

Walnuts, honey, a bit of crumbly cheese,

Propontis, the marble tower, a mosaic leopard

chewing on a guy's neck, the parakeets

in the palace trees, the old public wash basins

for ablutions, the big exfoliating silk glove

of the man who scraped the dead skin off my back,

a catalog of distant stones; don't worry, the old poets

skipped over plague years, too: poppies

That one carves the air to a mythic slash

in tones, chords; lives on striped nerves,

public scars. The moon needed a brother

to help spread dust over the city at midnight

one no pain, curse, or dishonesty could mark

no finger to touch a calloused sleeve

with no word to leave; lit up from behind

he calls me bad names from beyond the door

Vertigo, Iago, processed food for snacks.

With the angry innocence of a smoke ring

I carry the force of air, in and out, TINY COPS

some hiss flies above us, CORONAL MASS EJECTION

helicopter, military transport, irradiated cows

weird goop on the trees, gentle but yearsucked

been home so long

I'm not looking for a reason

It's a rough style of shame

to kill what can't be imagined

Tuesdays in 2061

the war on January

fire against star

out past the proving ground

not even an exploding stone

can prop open the earth

Assess the curriculum of smoke

in a halo of pine-scented oils:

it's lux, billows up the oiled light

drifts into the leg hair, lux, deluxe.

It would be kinda delicious if you

could teach the odd powers

of weather to flame and lick up. Ugh

those old noises. Scorched. Again and again

When emptiness is an island of dawn activity

far within other worlds, small other worlds

longer than the twist of an arm

heavier than a flick of hands

a wind presses over the crest like an old sweet reed

with a twist of ceremonial feeling

this desert is more than a luxurious mound

feathery, extravagant, glossed around by the wind

But it's only so much pocked stone and rust

edged and opened into this pale drift and crest

and I love it for that, for turning outward

coiled and smoothed into lean, temporary shapes

in its own time, a 'delicious solitude'

—the mound speaks low tones you can touch

something something reverent, something gusts

and all creation fades to voice

Something something something

jokey and nervous about curved emptiness.

The bumps hesitations and obstacles

keep you hearing, though a heap

doesn't resound, echo, or move like stone

into the wind-drift just to catch this unserious wind-grace

the billow on a page drifts in, pushes tiny stones together

placed upon your solace: a dry thought in no shade

It gets all over like dog hair, the sun

and it smells like Marlboro Lights in this port-a-potty

a baseless waft, a mountain of sand; your restless shape

cupped by all the places a grain finds to rest

the high haze, the urging winds whistle in a Silver Bullet can

a certain graininess to the photo plus a little human

all the places it finds to fit into, some life

returns on the dust of a stranger

I tell you for true, there's no name to this place

the "middle of nowhere" rattles in through my pores

a little catch howls in the breath

tumbles down the brink

down the side of its windward slope

what I mean is specks

gusted up against the drift

on top of the speechless howl is a mountain

Or a pile, or a sift, a few arcing, languid tracks

leading in one ear and out the other

dust gets on your lips

"an old and solemn harmony"

badwater…sweetwater…battery acid…

hair all mussed up

when some human ears get too full of quiet

they get this *I gotta make a noise and run over something* feeling

And the dune moans along

flees and re-forms, sifts

(whatever shape it can handle)

a good place to hide out but don't get lazy

did you see that scattering of smallness

those swerves of dusty

curved against the sky

piled up against the oncoming morning

Dust carried across continents

in the hand or in the upper atmosphere

trembles apart on the surface of the sea

when I want to learn a strewn lesson

I walk away from your human, my human

the anger and confused, shameful grief

straight into the intelligible joy of a skunk

an old sweet song, a quivering stench

I put a fig in the wound

three genera of American cuckoo

a river scene flows under a scab

milkweed and wild

rose in a burn scar. Oops,

light comes out of the sun.

What a sheltering power: slit of grief

cut by the window

Out here in the thunderous blue

it's all cold ozone: A lily an' a fern,

drips of heart-blood on the path

gray-brown dots on a spotted petal.

We wait for the smoke to clear

wiggle like songbirds in the rain

put an apt fruit on a bizarre tongue:

you're one of my kind

It no longer snows in this country.

So what. You found a secret stair

opening on a drought-garden

some pebbles tossed

in the desert roses, semi-wilted

wonderful, yellowed, well, you know

suffering to cover the suffering.

It no longer snows in this country

Shearwaters off the coast

of a new green Antarctica

a swarm of tender, indifferent greetings

microscopic fuzz in the spume

fate swarms the whole

everything's gone sea-surface gray

I bet you could be glad in a halo of rough seas

off green cliffs, sea-wrack for an adjacent world

Road closed at Hogback

hazelnut crème on my numb spot

the disaster next to the picturesque

some creature tries to nest in that shit

early heat drips plant sweat on a scrub oak

OK! You yell and become a sanctified thing!

waterbirds sleep in the mown grass

orange moon nudges the play structure

In a video game called *Nothing Quest*

you go to a hidden land and push a feeling-shaped button and

your adversaries are certain friends in certain hours with different shadows.

The goal is to redraw a glyph in a decades-old book

to read exquisite patterns on a wall in ruins, etc. Or nothing at all.

The sun is behind you in the glass, your hair has a hint of auburn,

and when you run out of time, we chant your name

the way it's pronounced on this side

In the arrogant blue of this abstraction

we'll hold fast 'til you bring us

some polychrome business

for our staring pleasure, a colorful activity

or maybe a blue one, a light breeze devoid of pests

water evaporating off dirt

just so people like me can grin again

in a sun, worn out but familiar

The poems stray at the mention of hymns and anthems

the wind from the north has a nutty flavor

that's the non-technical language of fire

the meticulous teasing of air by inhalation

apocalypse for dummies, the air inside a joke

impossible or just difficult, like fig growing in Ontario

I greet you in the place of the seekers: a hum, not a place

the taste of dust passes over the tongue

Why even talk about the sea's death

fool's gold and pollen shimmer in the wave

the river squeezed out of a mountain

came to rest under this smoky fuck-all.

Let's split the roof of heaven to the very star

say something reasonable that you can agree with

squirt a dream on an echo, sea-warped and wooden,

an accurate portrait of somebody you used to know

Sunland hollows

a mellow hole in a labyrinth

with a tender shade that falls

all up on you, standing there

cold and deft

with a shimmer of expertise

the sweat on your lip is so tough

natural as the day you were born

The outrageous pretense at the center of your quivering, substantial privacy

I think of it and feel free, something empty fills with warm water,

then a jerk spews needy chaos all over the carpet in a hall of fame's lobby.

But all that disappears behind a glistening sheet of plastic

when I train my ear on the center of your diaphanous notions.

My man, you say, *let's eat something off the ground, let's take the poison path*

we'll let everybody know we carry answers to certain secrets.

There once there was an ocean, we said. A couple children looked at us

Scorpius Tactical and Maccabee Arms Ltd.

are sold out of machine guns—

utopia for a couple days.

Warm, evil, and meditative

I brush a little skull ring from my heart

in the window, police compare

the gold bits on their uniforms

tickle each other on the ribs

Wild rose energy

desert peach steadfastness

seemed like a permanent mood

a lick, a riff, a run, and then

the austere violence

in a sculpted marble knife

 rubbed free of decorative paint

scratches a passing shape in the sand

All this room in time

things I learn in my house

some people dream of private music

tunes the size of rooms

conditions slap you

spider guts on the glue gun

breathtaking little supernatural character

the singing's bad but I like the words

As a slip of distance, too sexy for a book

do unequivocal things and lilt in silence.

Even though a used feeling wiggles the air,

the purple air, the green, soak up the color

of clouds and rain in old technicolor movies

quiver like scum under twitching insects:

a schematic drawing of the motif

plus the ongoing question of spirit

Within earshot of the monastics

I die to pause, to be held, caressed,

the subject of resplendent gossip

whispered through the cup

of their many-practiced hands

as thunderstorm and fireworks

come in green shadows and sketch

wobbly light in spider's silk

Salt water and warm beer

in the fibers of your flannel

smells good on the ride home

out here in the skunks and treebark

all hands rub the pouchy flap of a Sunday

just flippity floppity standing there

with a red stripe across my forehead.

The captive angel runs through the trees

Whoever drove the car while we slept left

one telltale stain on the ceiling and tore

a pink chunk of foam from the seat. Hope it

felt good to carom off the pain of matter, hope

cottonwood fluff and streetlamp heat made a dent, hope

all the cunning blue that kept you down in these weeks

flaked off like paint on the curb outside the donut shoppe, made

the tires scream and pirouette: the glass came this close to your nose

After an infinite season

in a city of few trees

the volume knob ripens

this tragedy to a soaring wound.

There are other worlds next to our fingers

½ wind, ½ budded leaf, all werewolf

green upon the beloved mountain

all creation fades to voice

A king wants to slit the clouds with his fingernail

I teach the kid to eat tubers and avoid roads

it won't help when things get serious

snow melts in the gaps between pavers

we touch the ground like that, a faint scent (cool)

born in peacetime, fooled by permanence

let's point a phone at the planets

flies press their bodies against the valley floor

ACKNOWLEDGEMENTS

Parts of *So Tough* first appeared in *Oversound, Couplet Poetry, Posit, Folder Magazine, Nevada Historical Society Quarterly, VOLT, and Mercury Firs*. Thanks to the editors of these journals. Thanks to Collateral & Co. Dance Company for commissioning the section which begins "When an emptiness is an island of dawn activity" and ends "piled up against the oncoming morning".

Love to this book's first readers: John Coletti, AB Gorham, Lauren Levin, Lara Mimosa Montes, Meredith Oda, Cedar Sigo, and Alli Warren, and to Eleanor, Meredith, Felicia, Emily, Stephanie, David, Alana, Austin, Julia, Matt, Sameer, Nilo, Catherine, Sandra, Ragini, Chris, Steve, Ann, Claire, Casey, Dan, Stanleys, Odas, wonderful students, Club Confetti (Berrigan, Brown, Coletti, Dahl, Kahn, Larsen, Resnikoff), SJ, Gillian, Rebecca, MC, Ian, Bill, Susan, Sam, Liz, Brian, Laura, Mark Hirose, Cole, Tyrone, Brenda.

"I open the book and feel fear" incorporates snippets of interviews with Kristi Williams, Arzu Ozkal, and Mary Cale Wilson as part of the exhibition *La Jolla Reading Room*, Athenaeum Music and Arts Library, La Jolla, CA, Jan 14th-Mar 23rd, 2022.

Thank you: Roberto Tejada, Timothy Liu, Rebecca Lauren, Caitlyn Galloway.

To JC, SF, MH, and in memory of SC.

ABOUT THE AUTHOR

Jared Stanley is a poet who often works with artists and sometimes writes in prose. He is the author of four books of poetry, *So Tough*, *EARS*, *The Weeds*, and *Book Made of Forest*. He lives in Reno, Nevada and teaches at the University of Nevada, Reno.

Also by Jared Stanley

The Blurry Hole and Other Stories (with Sameer Farooq)
EARS
Shall
Ignore the Cries of Empty Stones and Your Flesh Will Break Out in Scavengers
The Weeds
Book Made of Forest
The Outer Bay

So Tough is printed in Adobe Garamond Pro.

www.saturnaliabooks.org